SCIENCE PROJECTS

Weather

Joel Rubin

Heinemann
LIBRARY

www.heinemann.co.uk/library

Visit our website to find out more information about Heinemann Library books.

To order:

☎ Phone 44 (0)1865 888066

▤ Send a fax to 44 (0)1865 314091

▢ Visit the Heinemann Library Bookshop at www.heinemann.co.uk/library to browse our catalogue and order online.

First published in Great Britain by Heinemann Library, Halley Court, Jordan Hill, Oxford OX2 8EJ, part of Harcourt Education. Heinemann Library is a registered trademark of Harcourt Education Ltd.

Produced for Harcourt Education by White-Thomson Publishing Ltd. Bridgewater Business Centre, 210 High Street, Lewes, East Sussex BN7 2NH

Editorial: Brian Fitzgerald
Design: Tim Mayer and Alison Walper
Illustrations: Cavedweller Studio
Picture Research: Amy Sparks
Production: Duncan Gilbert

Originated by Modern Age
Printed and bound in China by Leo Paper Group

ISBN 978 0 431 04043 1
12 11 10 09 08
10 9 8 7 6 5 4 3 2 1

British Library Cataloguing in Publication Data
Rubin, Joel
Weather. – (Science projects)
551.6
A full catalogue record for this book is available from the British Library.

Acknowledgements
The author and publishers are grateful to the following for permission to reproduce copyright material: Corbis/Daniel Aguilar/Reuters, **p. 8**; iStockphoto.com, **title page, pp. 32**, (Monte Wilson), **6** (Panagiotis Karageorgakis), **12** (Fabio Bustamante), **20** (Shane Link), **24** (Sergey Dubrovskiy), **28** (Volodymyr Kyrylyuk), **30tl** (Norbert – Zsolt Suto), **30tr** (Amy Walters), **30br, 36** (Andrew Penner), **39** (Jacob Carroll), **40** (Stephen Brake), **41** (Ashok Rodrigues); Masterfile/Andrew Douglas, **p. 4**; National Oceanic and Atmospheric Administration/ Department of Commerce, **pp. 16, 30bl** (Ralph F. Kresge)

Cover photograph reproduced with permission of Visuals Unlimited/Corbis

The publishers would like to thank Sue Glass for her assistance in the preparation of this book.

Every effort has been made to contact copyright holders of any material reproduced in this book. Any omissions will be rectified in subsequent printings if notice is given to the publishers.

Contents

» Any words appearing in bold, **like this,** are explained in the glossary.

Starting your science investigation

A science investigation is an exciting challenge. It starts with an idea that you can test by doing experiments. These are often lots of fun to do. But it is no good just charging in without planning first. A good scientist knows that they must first research their idea thoroughly, work out how they can test it, and plan their experiments carefully. When they have done these things, they can happily carry out their experiments to see if their idea is right.

Your experiments might support your original idea or they might shoot it down in flames. This doesn't matter. The important thing is that you will have found out a bit more about the world around you, and had fun along the way. You will be a happy scientist!

In this book, you'll look at nine science investigations relating to weather. You'll be able to discover some wonderful things about the world you live in.

Do your research

Is there something about weather and climate you've always wondered about? Something you don't quite understand but would like to? Then do a little research about the subject. Go to the library and find some books about the subject. Books written for students are often a very good place to start.

Use your favourite Internet search engine to find reliable online resources. Websites written by museums, universities, newspapers, and scientific journals are among the best sources for **accurate** research. Each investigation in this book has some suggestions for further research.

You need to make sure that your resources are reliable when doing research. Ask yourself the following questions, especially about the resources you find online.

The investigations   Background information

The start of each investigation contains a box like this.

Possible question

This question is a suggested starting point for your investigation. You will need to adapt the question to suit the things that interest you.

Possible hypothesis

This is only a suggestion. Don't worry if your hypothesis doesn't match the one listed here. Use your imagination!

Approximate cost of materials

Discuss this with your parents before starting work. Don't spend too much.

Materials needed

Make sure you can easily get all of the materials listed and gather them together before starting work.

Level of difficulty

There are three levels of investigations in this book: Easy, Intermediate, and Advanced. The level of difficulty is based on how long the investigation takes and how complicated it is.

1) How old is the resource? Is the information up to date or is it very old?

2) Who wrote the resource? Is the author identified so you know who they are, and what qualifies them to write about the topic?

3) What is the purpose of the resource? A website from a business or pressure group might not give balanced information, but one from a university probably will.

4) Is the information well documented? Can you tell where the author got their information from so you can check how accurate it is?

Some websites allow you to "chat" online with experts. Make sure you discuss this with a parent or teacher first. Never give out personal information online. The "Think U Know" website at http://www.thinkuknow.co.uk has loads of tips about safety online.

Once you know a little more about the subject you want to investigate, you'll be ready to work out your scientific question. You will be able to use this to make a sensible **hypothesis**. A hypothesis is an idea about why something happens that can be tested by doing experiments. Finally, you'll be ready to begin your science investigation!

A flash of lightning is one of the most dramatic events in nature. In this book, you'll learn how lightning and other weather events occur.

What is an experiment?

Often when someone says that they are going to do an experiment, they mean they are just going to fiddle with something to see what happens. But scientists mean something else. They mean that they are going to control the **variables** involved in a careful way. A variable is something that changes or can be changed. Independent variables are things that you deliberately keep the same or change in your experiment. You should always aim to keep all the independent variables constant, except for the one you are investigating. The dependent variable is the change that happens because of the one independent variable that you do change. You make a fair test if you set up your experiment so that you only change one independent variable at a time. Your results are valid if you have carried out a fair test, and recorded your results or observations honestly.

Sometimes you might want to compare one group with another to see what happens. For example, imagine you want to test whether sunlight will heat up a container of water. You place three bowls of water in sunlight (Group A). You leave three identical bowls of water in a shady place indoors (Group B). Group A is your test group and Group B is your **control**. You would be looking to see if there is a difference between the two groups. In this experiment, the location of the bowls is the independent variable, and the effect of sunlight on the water temperature is the dependent variable.

You must do experiments carefully so that your results are accurate and reliable. Ideally, you would get the same results if you did your investigation all over again.

Your hypothesis

Once you've decided on the question you're going to try to answer, you then make a scientific **prediction** of what you'll find out in your science project.

For example, if you wonder whether the types of clouds you see in the sky have any effect on the weather, your question might be, "Do different types of clouds give clues about the weather?" Remember, a hypothesis is an idea about why something happens, which can be tested by doing experiments. So your hypothesis in response to the above question might be, "The types of clouds we see give clues about the weather." With a hypothesis, you can also work out if you can actually do the experiments needed to answer your question. Think of a question like: "How many raindrops fall during a thunderstorm?" It would be impossible to support your hypothesis, however you express it. So, be sure you can actually get the **evidence** needed to support or disprove your hypothesis.

Keeping records

Good scientists keep careful notes in their lab book about everything they do. This is really important. Other scientists may want to try out the experiments to see if they get the same results. So the records in your lab book need to be clear and easy to follow. What sort of things should you write down?

It is a good idea to write some notes about the research you found in books and on websites. You should also include the names of the books or the web addresses. This will save you from having to find these useful resources all over again later. You should also write down your hypothesis and your reasons for it. All your **data** and results should go into your lab book, too.

Your results are the evidence that you use to make your conclusion. Never rub out an odd-looking result or tweak it to "look right". An odd result may turn out to be important later. You should write down *every* result you get. Tables are a really good way to record lots of results clearly. Make sure you record when you did your experiments, and anything you might have changed along the way to improve them. No detail is too small when it comes to scientific research.

There are tips for making a great report with each investigation and at the end of this book. Use them as guides and don't be afraid to be creative. Make it *your* investigation!

The pressure is on

Although you can't feel it, the weight of the air around us is constantly pressing down on Earth. This is called **air pressure.** It plays a key role in predicting weather: High pressure usually means cool, clear weather; low pressure can bring clouds, rain, even hurricanes (above). **Meteorologists,** scientists who study weather, use an instrument called a **barometer** to measure air pressure. Build a barometer of your own and start measuring weather the way the professionals do.

Do your research

This project involves making a barometer and using it to monitor changes in air pressure. Before you get started, do some research on air pressure systems and find out more about barometers and how they work. Then you can either make the barometer described in this project or come up with a design of your own.

Here is a book and some websites you could start with in your research:

» *Measuring the Weather: Wind and Air Pressure*, Alan Rodgers and Angella Streluk (Heinemann, 2007)

Background information

Possible question

Can a homemade barometer accurately measure changes in air pressure?

Possible hypothesis

A homemade barometer will correctly show increases and decreases in air pressure.

Level of difficulty

Intermediate

Approximate cost of materials

£6.00

Materials needed

» A balloon
» Scissors
» Empty wide-mouthed jar, such as a mayonnaise or pickle jar
» Elastic band (optional)
» Drinking straw
» Sticky tape
» Ruler
» Sheet of paper

» Air pressure
http://www.srh.noaa.gov/jetstream/atmos/pressure.htm
» It's a breeze: How air pressure affects you
http://kids.earth.nasa.gov/archive/air_pressure/index.html

Outline of methods

1. Cut the balloon at its neck and throw the neck away. Stretch the balloon over the opening of the jar. The balloon should be tight like the cover of a drum. If you have trouble fitting the balloon over the jar yourself, ask a helper to hold the jar as you stretch the balloon over the jar's opening. Make sure the seal is tight – you don't want any air to escape from the jar. If necessary, secure the balloon in place with sticky tape or an elastic band.

2. Tape one end of the straw to the middle of the "drum".

3. Use the ruler to mark lines ½ centimetre (0.2 inch) apart on the sheet of paper.

Continued

4. Tape the sheet of paper to a wall and position the barometer on a flat surface in front of it. Angle the barometer so the straw is close to the wall but not touching it.

5. Check the barometric reading for your area on a weather website. Write the reading next to the mark on the paper that is even with the top of the straw. Also record the reading in your lab book and make notes about the weather conditions at the time you took the reading.

6. Take readings twice a day. High pressure will cause the balloon on your barometer to be pushed in and the straw to rise slightly. Low pressure will cause the balloon to bulge out and the straw to point down (see illustration). Use the weather website to check your barometer's changes against those of the air pressure in your area. Record the actual readings along with the weather conditions in your lab book.

7. Continue to take and record readings for one week.

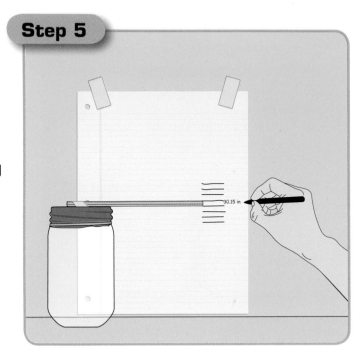

Step 5

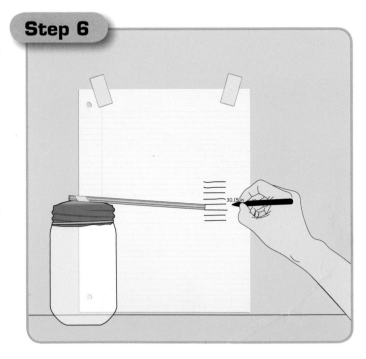

Step 6

Analysis of results

» Did the reading on your barometer change at each observation?

» Did you notice the top of your barometer bulging out or being pushed in at certain readings?

» How did the changes in your barometer compare with the air pressure readings you found online?

» What changes did you notice in the weather as your barometer rose and fell?

More activities to extend your investigation

» Once you've tested your barometer for a few days, stop comparing your readings with those online. Continue to record the rise and fall of your barometer, and then make weather predictions based on your research.

» Do more research and make other weather instruments – you can build a whole weather station!

Project extras

» Research and present the history of the barometer.

» Photograph your homemade barometer and include these photographs along with photographs of a real barometer in your report.

» Research and report the historic high and low barometric pressure readings for your region.

The warm and cold of it

Heat from the sun warms Earth's air, water, and land – but air, water, and land gain and lose heat at very different rates. This creates differences in temperature. Warm air rises and expands, and cooler air moves in to take its place. The result is wind. Temperature differences between land and sea can create everything from a pleasant sea breeze to a deadly hurricane. Which material loses heat the fastest? Find out with this "cool" project!

Do your research

This project explores how air, water, and land change temperatures at different rates. You will need to use a refrigerator, so make sure you get your parents' permission before you start. Begin by doing some research on the **heat capacity** of air, water, and land and the role it plays in the formation of wind, breezes, hurricanes, and other types of extreme weather. Once you've done some research, you can tackle this project or create your own version.

Here is a book and some websites you could start with in your research:

» *Eyewitness: Weather*, Brian Cosgrove (Dorling Kindersley, 2004)
» Heat capacity
  http://www.exploratorium.edu/climate/glossary/heat-capacity.html

Background information

Possible question

Which loses heat the fastest – air, water, or soil?

Possible hypothesis

Air loses heat faster than both soil and water do.

Level of difficulty

Easy

Approximate cost of materials

£8.00

Materials needed

» Three identical thermometers
» Three plastic cups
» Room-temperature water
» Potting soil or sand from a newly opened bag, enough to fill one plastic cup halfway
» Plate or tray large enough to hold three plastic cups
» Refrigerator

» Land and sea breeze activity: http://www.classzone.com/books/earth_science/terc/content/visualizations/es1903/es1903page01.cfm
» The sea breeze
http://www.ace.mmu.ac.uk/eae/Weather/Older/Sea_Breeze.html

Outline of methods

1. Set up a data table in your lab book like the one shown below.

Step 1

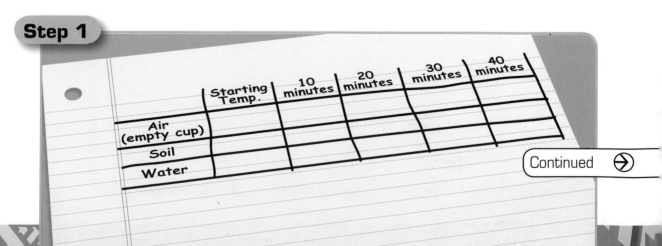

	Starting Temp.	10 minutes	20 minutes	30 minutes	40 minutes
Air (empty cup)					
Soil					
Water					

Continued →

2. Fill one cup about halfway with soil and another to the same level with water. Leave the third cup empty – it will hold only air.

3. Place one thermometer upright in each cup. Push the bulb of the thermometer down into the soil. You will need to see enough of the thermometer in the soil to read the range between room and refrigerator temperature.

4. Allow enough time for the air, water, and soil to reach the same temperature.

5. Place all three cups on a plate or tray in the refrigerator.

Step 5

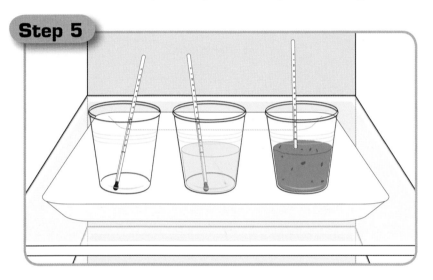

6. Read and record the cup temperatures at 10-minute intervals. Make sure you close the refrigerator door while waiting so you don't waste electricity.

7. Stop when the temperature in each of the three cups does not change for three readings in a row.

Analysis of results

» Did the air, water, and soil change temperature at the same rate?

» If not, which material changed temperature the fastest?

» Which material changed temperature the slowest?

More activities to extend your investigation

» Extend the experiment by removing the three cups from the refrigerator and placing them on a table or work surface at room temperature. Record the rate at which the temperature of the material in each cup increases.

» Using the same set-up, place the cups under a desk lamp rather than in the refrigerator. Make sure each cup gets an equal amount of light. Take readings every five minutes to determine whether water, air, or soil absorbs heat the fastest. The lamp acts like the sun heating Earth's oceans (the cup of water) and land (the cup of soil).

» Repeat the experiment using other materials, such as wet and dry clay. Use a wooden skewer or the sharp end of a compass to make a hole for the thermometer in two lumps of wet clay. Allow one lump to dry, and then place thermometers in both. Place both lumps on a tray in the refrigerator and compare the rate at which the temperature decreases in each.

» Use your knowledge of weather and your research data to explain how land and water temperature differences affect weather as wind moves from ocean to land.

Project extras

» Display your data using a colour code, such as red to purple to blue, to represent the temperature change from warm to cold over the time interval you selected.

» Include an illustrated explanation of how hurricanes quickly lose energy after they leave the ocean and begin travelling over land.

» Display photographs taken from space that show the difference between ocean surface temperature and wind direction and the temperature and wind direction on land.

Moving heat

The previous activity ("The warm and cold of it") showed that air, land, and water change temperature at different rates. The continuous rising of hot air and sinking of cooler air created by these temperature differences is called **convection.** This process also creates ocean currents, such as the Gulf Stream, which has a major effect on the climate of Europe and North America. (The Gulf Stream is shown above in red and orange along the east coast of the United States.) In this project, you'll create a convection current using coloured water in an aquarium.

Do your research

Convection is the transfer of heat through the movement of a liquid (such as water) or a gas (such as air). For this experiment, you'll use water to demonstrate how hot and cold fluids move in a convection current. Before beginning this project, do some research on convection to find out more about how this process affects weather. Then you can try this activity or come up with a version all of your own.

Background information

Possible question

What happens when both hot and cold water are added to a container of water?

Possible hypothesis

The hot water will rise to the top of the container, and the cold water will sink to the bottom.

Level of difficulty

Intermediate

Approximate cost of materials

£10.00

Materials needed

» Room-temperature and hot water
» Freezer and ice cube tray
» Blue food colouring
» Small plastic aquarium or other clear container
» Red food colouring
» Bulb-type meat baster
» Clock or stopwatch

Here is a book and some websites you could start with in your research:

» *Weather and Climate: Atmosphere and Weather*, Terry Jennings (Evans Brothers, 2005)
» NASA: For kids only: Earth science enterprise http://kids.earth.nasa.gov/facts.htm
» Convection: http://www.think-energy.com/ThinkEnergy/11-14/activities/ConvectionCurrents.aspx

Outline of methods

1. The night before you do this project, fill an ice cube tray with water and add a few drops of blue food colouring to two or three of the cubes. (You'll need only one ice cube for the experiment, but it's a good idea to make extras.)

Continued

2. Fill the aquarium or other container three-quarters full with room-temperature water.

3. Mix a few drops of red food colouring into a cup of hot water.

4. Carefully fill the meat baster with the hot red water.

5. Drop a blue ice cube into one end of the aquarium.

6. Insert the meat baster into the aquarium on the side opposite the ice cube. Put the tip of the baster as close to the bottom of the aquarium as possible and squirt a small amount of red water into the tank.

Step 6

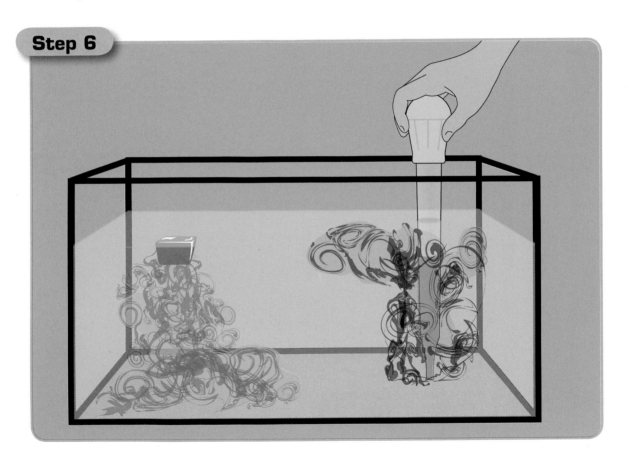

7. Observe and record the movement of the water until it stops moving and the colours are blended. This will take a few minutes.

Analysis of results

» Did the warm water rise to the top of the aquarium? If so, how long did that take?

» Did the ice melt and sink to the bottom of the aquarium? If so, how long did that take?

» How long did it take the colours to mix completely?

More activities to extend your investigation

» Expand the project by clamping a small aquarium heater to one end of your aquarium. Use two clothes pegs to clamp a soft ice pack at the other end. Then follow steps 2 to 6 from the project. Observe how the water moves around the aquarium.

» Take photos of the rising and falling of the coloured hot and cold water in your aquarium. Include the photos in your report.

Project extras

» Include pictures or illustrations with arrows that show convection currents in action, such as steam rising from a bowl of soup.

» Include a diagram that explains how convection currents act as a conveyor belt that affects weather and climate in your region by moving hot and cold masses of air and water.

It's raining indoors

How is it possible that rivers constantly flow into oceans and centimetres and centimetres of rain fall each year, yet the land isn't completely covered with water? All of the water on Earth and in the **atmosphere** is constantly recycled through the **water cycle** – a process that is vital for the survival of all living things. In this project, you'll use only a few household items to re-create the water cycle.

Do your research

This project deals with the water cycle – the process by which water goes from a solid or liquid to water vapour and back again. Before you start, do some research to find out more about the key parts of the water cycle: **evaporation, condensation, precipitation,** and **collection.** Then see the water cycle in action using this project or a similar project you design yourself.

Here are some books and websites where you can begin your research:

» *Studying Weather*, Ted O'Hare (Rourke Publishing, 2003)

» *The Water Cycle*, Trudi Strain Trueit (Franklin Watts, 2002)

» Animated diagram of the water cycle
   http://www.bbc.co.uk/schools/riversandcoasts/water_cycle/rivers/index.shtml

Background information

Possible question

Can "rain" be made indoors?

Possible hypothesis

Rain can be made indoors by placing a sealed bag of ice over a container of hot water.

Level of difficulty

Easy

Approximate cost of materials

£0.00

Materials needed

» Tall clear jug or another clear container, such as an empty 2-litre drinks bottle cut at the shoulder
» Hot water
» Large resealable plastic bag filled with ice
» Clock or watch

» The water cycle: http://www.naturegrid.org.uk/rivers/watercyclepages/watercycle-intro.html
» The water cycle: http://ga.water.usgs.gov/edu/watercycle.html

Outline of methods

1. Carefully fill the container about one-quarter full with hot water.

2. Place the sealed ice-filled plastic bag on top of the jug, making sure the opening is completely covered. The sides of the container should fog up a bit almost immediately. Place the ice-covered jug in direct sunlight.

3. Record how long it takes for droplets of water (condensation) to form on the bottom of the bag. This will take a few minutes.

Continued

Step 3

4. Record how long it takes before the droplets start to fall into the container.

5. Continue to observe the container for 10 minutes after the first droplet falls. Count the total number of droplets that fall into the container.

6. Repeat the experiment at least two times and compare the results from each test.

The Water Cycle

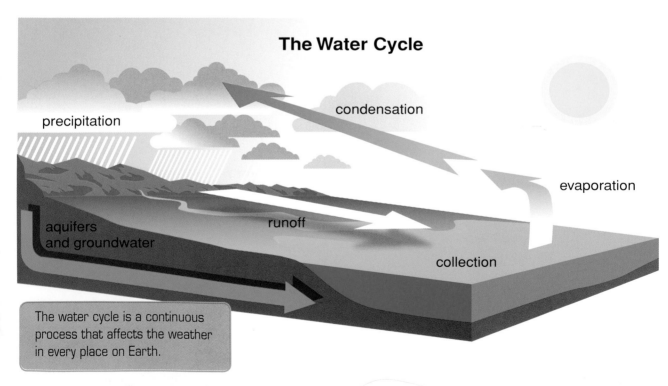

precipitation

condensation

evaporation

aquifers and groundwater

runoff

collection

The water cycle is a continuous process that affects the weather in every place on Earth.

Analysis of results

» How long did it take for droplets to form on the bottom of the ice-filled bag?

» How long did it take before the droplets increased in size and then fell like rain?

» Did each test produce the same results? If not, what variables might have affected the results?

More activities to extend your investigation

» Repeat the project using more, and then less, hot water in the container. Does this affect the amount of time it takes for condensation to appear?

» Add food colouring to the water to test whether the water droplets will be coloured or clear.

» Add salt to the water and taste whether the water droplets that form on the bag are salty or fresh.

Project extras

» Include rain photographs and draw a poster illustrating the water cycle.

» Research which areas of the world get the most and least rainfall. Use your knowledge of the water cycle to explain why.

Cloud in a container

Many clouds *look* like they're made of big, fluffy cotton wool balls. But anyone who has ever walked through fog knows that it *feels* like it's made mostly of wet, cold air. This project will show you how to make your own cloud in a matter of a few minutes.

Do your research

For this project, you'll create a cloud using a similar set-up to the one used in the previous project ("It's raining indoors"). You'll need a lit match to make the experiment work, so ask an adult to help you. Before you begin, research clouds and how they form. Then you can either try this activity or put your own unique spin on it.

Here is a book and some websites you could start with in your research:

» *Measuring the Weather: Cloud Cover*, Alan Rodgers and Angella Streluk (Heinemann, 2007)

» NASA space place: Let's find out more about clouds!
http://spaceplace.jpl.nasa.gov/en/kids/cloudsat_puz3.shtml

Background information

Possible question

Is it possible to make a cloud?

Possible hypothesis

Clouds can be made using a few simple materials.

Level of difficulty

Intermediate

Approximate cost of materials

£0.00

Materials needed

» Tall clear jug or another clear container, such as an empty 2-litre drinks bottle cut at the shoulder
» Hot water
» Large resealable plastic bag filled with ice
» Match
» Sheet of black paper
» Clock or watch
» Sticky tape (optional)
» Adult supervisor

» Clouds: http://www.metoffice.gov.uk/education/primary/students/clouds.html
» Fog: http://www.bbc.co.uk/weather/features/understanding/fog.shtml

Outline of methods

1. Carefully fill the container about one-quarter full with hot water.

2. Place the sealed ice-filled plastic bag on top of the container, making sure the opening is completely covered. The sides of the container should fog up a bit almost immediately.

3. Record how long it takes for droplets of water to form on the bottom of the bag. This will take a few minutes.

4. Once water droplets begin to form on the bottom of the bag of ice, ask your adult helper to light the match and then blow it out.

ADULT SUPERVISION REQUIRED

Continued

5. Quickly lift the bag of ice from the top of the container and drop the still-smoking match into the container.

6. Replace the bag of ice immediately.

7. Hold the black paper behind the container, or tape it to a wall behind the container. This will allow you to see the cloud more clearly. Record how long it takes for the container to start to get cloudy.

8. Remove the bag of ice to allow the cloud to escape from the container. Note how the cloud feels on your hands and face.

9. Repeat the experiment at least two times and compare the results from each test.

Step 7

Analysis of results

» How long did it take for a cloud to form?

» What did the cloud feel like?

» How long did it take for the cloud to disappear?

» Did each test produce the same results? If not, what variables might have affected the results?

More activities to extend your investigation

» Add red or blue food colouring to the water and see whether it creates a coloured cloud.

» For a different view of your cloud, try the activity in a darkened room and shine a torch on the container.

» Research and report on cloud seeding and how it is used to create rain.

Project extras

» Include photographs of clouds and fog.

» Take photographs of your experimental set-up and include them in your report.

Sky watch

You've probably seen all types of shapes in clouds – an elephant, a castle, maybe even your favourite cartoon character. But did you know that you're also seeing clues about what the weather will be later? Cumulus clouds are known as "fair-weather clouds". Other types, such as nimbus clouds, bring rain or snow. If you'd like to predict the weather by watching the clouds, this project will show you how.

Do your research

For this project, you will observe the types of clouds in the sky and note the weather that follows. Give yourself plenty of time. You'll need to observe a few different cloud types and different weather conditions. Before you start, do some research on the different types of clouds. Then you can tackle this project. Or, you may come up with your own unique project after you've learned more.

Here is a book and some websites that can help you get started:

» *Cloud Dance*, Thomas Locker (Voyager, 2003)
» BBC weather: Types of clouds
   http://www.bbc.co.uk/weather/features/weatherbasics/cloud_types.shtml
» S'COOL: On-line cloud chart
   http://asd-www.larc.nasa.gov/SCOOL/cldchart.html
» Jetstream: An online school for weather: Clouds
   http://www.srh.noaa.gov/jetstream/synoptic/clouds.htm

Background information

Possible question

Can you predict the weather by observing clouds?

Materials needed

» A cloud chart (can be found online at sites such as http://asd-www.larc.nasa.gov/SCOOL/cldchart.html)

Possible hypothesis

Clouds can tell us what type of weather to expect.

Level of difficulty

Easy

Approximate cost of materials

£0.00

Outline of methods

1. For each day that you plan to observe the sky, write the date at the top of a blank page in your lab book.

2. Divide each page into two sections – one for observations made in the morning and the other for observations in the afternoon.

Step 3

Date: 20 September

Morning

Cloud type(s): Stratus
Cloud cover: 100%; completely cloudy
Weather conditions: Cool, no wind
Prediction: cloudy skies, maybe some rain

Afternoon

Cloud type(s):
Cloud cover:
Weather conditions:
Prediction:

3. Add the following headings to both sections on the page: cloud types; **cloud cover** – the amount of the sky that is covered with clouds; weather conditions (hot, cold, sunny, raining, etc.); and your prediction for what the weather will be later in the day or the next day.

Continued

4. Observe the sky every morning. Compare the clouds in the sky with those on your cloud chart. You may see more than one type of cloud at a time. In your lab book, record the types of clouds you see and the cloud cover. Also record the weather and your prediction for the weather at your next observation. Follow the same procedure each afternoon.

5. Continue your observations for at least two weeks. You should observe each type of cloud, and the weather that follows it, more than once.

When you see cumulonimbus clouds, you can expect rain and thunder in the near future.

These are not pieces of cotton – they're cumulus clouds. These clouds are sometimes called "fair-weather clouds".

Is it a grey day? Low-lying stratus clouds are probably to blame. They often cover the entire sky.

High, wispy cirrus clouds are signs of pleasant weather. But expect a change in weather if they start to thicken.

Analysis of results

» Which types of clouds did you see most often?

» Did you correctly predict the weather conditions that followed each observation?

» Did you notice different types of clouds in the sky at the same time? If so, how did this seem to affect the type of weather that followed?

More activities to extend your investigation

» Take photographs of the sky during each observation.

» Carry out your investigation in the evening to see whether cloud types are the same when it is dark as they are when it is light. Never work outside alone in the dark – make sure that an adult comes with you.

» Research the Latin root words for the name of each cloud type. Explain how the Latin meanings give clues about what each type of cloud looks like.

Project extras

» Create a chart or graph that illustrates the number of days you saw each type of cloud. Include photographs of the various cloud types you observed.

Lightning strikes

Lightning is definitely one of Mother Nature's coolest tricks – an all-natural fireworks display. Do you want to see some sparks fly? You can create the conditions necessary to produce sparks of lightning right in your own home.

Do your research

For this project, you will build an **electrophorus** – a device that produces static electricity. You will find that it works best indoors during cold, dry weather and that it won't work at all if the weather is hot and humid. Before you begin, do some research on static electricity and how lightning is produced. Then you can either build this electrophorus or create your own static electricity generator.

Here is a book and some websites that will help with your research:

» *Lightning*, Seymour Simon (Harper Collins, 2006)

» What causes a lightning flash?
   http://ksnn.larc.nasa.gov/webtext.cfm?unit=lightning

» BBC Weather Centre: Lightning
   http://www.bbc.co.uk/weather/features/understanding/lightning.shtml

Background information

Possible question

What materials will create static electricity?

Possible hypothesis

Wool and other fabrics will create static electricity.

Level of difficulty

Intermediate

Approximate cost of materials

£1.50

Materials needed

» Drawing pin
» Disposable aluminium dish
» Pencil with a rubber
» Wool sock or mitten, or a scrap of wool fabric
» Polystyrene plate or a small block of polystyrene
» Scrap of leather (available at a fabric store)
» Light bulb

Outline of methods

1. Push the drawing pin through the centre of the aluminium dish.

Step 2

2. Push the rubber end of the pencil onto the drawing pin to create a handle.

3. Rub the sock or mitten quickly backwards and forwards over the polystyrene.

4. Pick up the dish by its handle and place it upside down on top of the polystyrene. The dish and polystyrene should stick together. You have just created an electrophorus.

Continued

5. Turn off the lights in the room and carefully touch your finger to the dish. You should see a spark and feel a little shock.

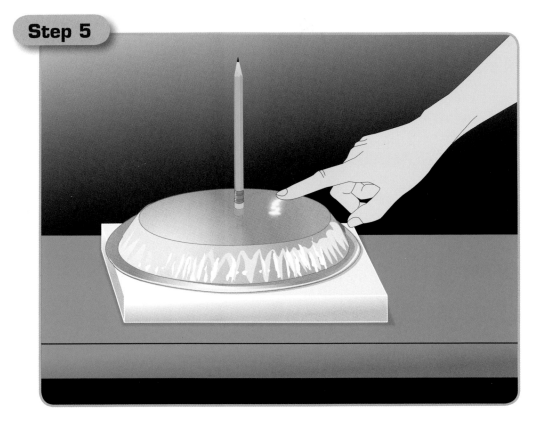

Step 5

6. Rate the shock and the spark on a scale of 1 (small) to 5 (large) in your lab book.

7. Repeat step 3, this time with the scrap of leather, and then repeat steps 4 to 6.

8. Repeat the test by rubbing the glass end of a light bulb over the polystyrene. Finally, test whether you get a shock after rubbing the polystyrene against your hair. Compare the shock and sparks generated by each object.

9. Repeat the experiment on each of the next two days. Compare the shock and sparks generated by each object on the different days.

Analysis of results

» Which material produced the biggest shock?

» Which material produced the biggest spark?

» Did any materials fail to produce a shock and spark? If so, why might that be?

» Were the results the same on different days? If not, what variables might have been involved?

More activities to extend your investigation

» Research and explain why this experiment will not work in hot, humid weather.

» Research Benjamin Franklin and other early scientists who studied electricity.

» After charging the electrophorus (step 4), bring a small fluorescent tube (the long, narrow light bulb tubes sometimes used in kitchen and shop lighting) near the aluminium dish. Touch one terminal of the tube with your finger and touch the terminal at the other end to the charged dish. The tube should briefly glow.

Project extras

» Take photographs of your electrophorus and include them in your report.

» Include some dramatic photos of lightning in your report.

Weather wise

Long before there were TV meteorologists, sailors, farmers, and other people who worked outdoors made weather predictions based on their experiences. Then they made up easy-to-remember sayings, or proverbs, about what they observed. How accurate are these sayings? You be the judge!

Do your research

This project involves testing the accuracy of weather sayings, such as "Red sky at night, shepherd's delight". Research weather sayings and the science behind them, and then pick one or two that you think you will be able to test. Bear in mind the time of the year and the type of weather in your region. (For example, if it's spring, don't pick a saying that relates to snow.) Plan to make daily observations for about a month. This should allow you to see many types of weather changes. Once you've read about popular sayings and what they mean, you can tackle this project or come up with one of your own.

Here is a book and some websites you could start with in your research:

» *The Old Farmer's Almanac* (Yankee Publishing, 1792–present)
» Weather lore
  http://www.coldal.org/weather.htm

Background information

Possible question

Do folk sayings provide useful advice about future weather events?

Materials needed

» Binder for collecting weather reports

Possible hypothesis

Yes, some folk sayings do provide useful advice about future weather events.

Level of difficulty

Intermediate

Approximate cost of materials

£0.00

» Weather sayings
http://www.metoffice.gov.uk/education/primary/students/sayings.html

» Weather wisdom
http://www.bbc.co.uk/dna/h2g2/A641305

Possible sayings to test

- Ring around the Moon, rain or snow will come soon.

- Red sky at night, shepherd's delight. Red sky in morning, shepherd's warning.

- Rain before seven, fine by eleven.

- A sun shiny shower, won't last half an hour.

- No weather is ill if the wind be still.

Outline of methods

1. Choose weather sayings that are appropriate to your area and the time of year. To increase your odds of seeing something, select more than one weather proverb to investigate. Weather patterns are different all over the world, so the weather described in some proverbs may not occur in your area. Many sayings are related to rain or other forms of precipitation – test these sayings during a month in which some rain is expected.

Continued

2. Research the science behind your selected sayings, using resources such as those included in "Do your research". The saying investigated here is "Ring around the Moon, rain or snow will come soon." Testing this saying requires some research into the phases of the Moon.

3. Check the weather forecast in a local newspaper or online. Save the daily weather forecast in your binder.

4. Observe the sky at the same time each night. Note what you see in a chart in your lab book, even if you don't see a ring around the Moon. Note the phases of the Moon and if any part of the Moon is covered by clouds. Also record the weather conditions.

Step 4

Date: 20 September

Morning weather: Cool, clear skies
Evening weather: Colder, clear skies
Phase of the Moon: First quarter
Ring around the Moon? No
Description of ring: N/A

5. Observe the weather the next morning and note the weather conditions in your lab book. If it's raining, note whether it's a drizzle, heavy rain, a steady rain all day, and so on.

6. Repeat steps 3 to 5 each night for a month.

7. On nights you observe a ring around the Moon, draw a picture of what you see in your lab book. Note how clearly you can see the ring and how thick it appears to be.

Analysis of results

» On how many nights did you see a ring around the Moon?

» Each time, did rain or snow follow the next day?

» Did you see any relationship between the thickness of the ring and the amount of rainfall or snowfall the next day?

» If you didn't see a ring around the Moon on any night, why might that be?

» Did it rain or snow on any days after you didn't see a ring around the Moon?

More activities to extend your investigation

» Take photos of the Moon on the nights that a ring appears. Create a chart that shows the level of rainfall on each of the days that follow.

» Based on your observations, try to come up with your own weather-related saying.

Project extras

» Include each day's weather forecasts that you collected.

» Create a poster that includes other well-known weather sayings alongside photos that show those weather events.

» Explain how some of the sayings are important to a particular person's work, such as a farmer or sailor.

Moonlight reflected from ice crystals high in Earth's atmosphere creates a ring around the Moon.

What's cooking?

You've probably heard people say it's hot enough outside to fry an egg – but is there any truth to the saying? Does the sun actually produce enough heat to cook food? This project will help you find out!

Do your research

For the best results, try this project on a warm sunny day between the hours of 10 a.m. and 2 p.m. Remember to wear sunscreen and never look directly at the sun. A solar oven can get very hot, so make sure an adult is present when you perform the project. Before you begin, do some research on the many ways in which the sun affects weather. You'll also need to learn about solar energy and solar cookers. Then you'll be ready to try this project or come up with one of your own.

Here is a book and some websites you could start with in your research:

» *Eyewitness: Weather*, Brian Cosgrove (Dorling Kindersley, 2004)
» Solar energy
   http://www.scienceonline.co.uk/energy/renewable-energy.html#solar
» Energy from the sun
   http://www.eia.doe.gov/kids/energyfacts/sources/renewable/solar.html

Background information

Possible question

Can heat from the sun's rays be used to cook food?

Possible hypothesis

Food can be cooked by trapping heat from the sun's rays in a solar oven.

Level of difficulty	Approximate cost of materials
Advanced	£7.00

Materials needed

» Empty pizza box
» Scissors
» Aluminium foil
» Glue
» Plastic oven bag
» Masking tape or duct tape
» Ingredients to make your "sandwich" snack: two biscuits, a chocolate bar, and marshmallows
» Oven thermometer
» Pencil or wooden skewer (optional)
» Spatula
» Oven gloves
» Adult supervisor

Your "sandwich" snack will be made of melted chocolate and marshmallows sandwiched between two biscuits.

Outline of methods

1. Draw a large square on the top of the pizza box, leaving a 2.5-centimetre (1-inch) border all around.

2. Cut along three sides of the square, leaving the line at the back of the box uncut.

ADULT SUPERVISION REQUIRED

3. Gently fold the cut cardboard top back at the uncut line to create a flap.

Continued

4. Cut a piece of aluminium foil to the size of the underside of the flap. Glue the foil in place, smoothing out any wrinkles.

5. Make a "window" in the pizza box by cutting a piece of the oven bag slightly larger than the hole in the top of the box. Tape the plastic in place on the underside of the hole. Make sure there are no gaps between the plastic and the sides of the box so heat can't escape.

6. Cut another piece of aluminium foil to the size of the inside of the pizza box. Glue it in place, smoothing out any wrinkles.

7. Assemble your sandwich. Put it and the oven thermometer on the foil in the box. Close the window.

8. Position the oven to face the sun. Make sure the aluminium-covered flap is folded back far enough to reflect the maximum amount of sunlight directly into the box. Prop the flap open with a pencil or skewer if necessary. Remember not to look directly at the sun.

9. Look through the window to take temperature readings and observe the sandwich every 10 minutes.

10. Once the chocolate is melted, use the spatula to remove the sandwich. The oven will be hot, so make sure you wear oven gloves.

Step 5

Step 8

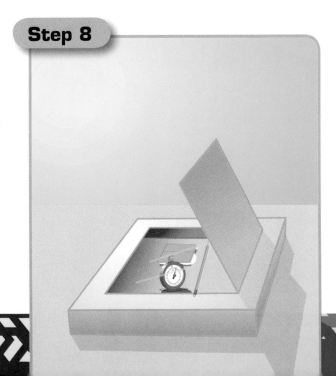

Analysis of results

» What was the maximum temperature the oven reached?

» How long did it take to reach the maximum temperature?

» How long did it take for the chocolate to melt?

» At what temperature did the chocolate melt?

More activities to extend your investigation

» Demonstrate how to make a solar cooker and provide a pattern and directions so that other students can make one at home.

» Try other dishes in your solar oven, such as cheese on toast. Record how long it takes for the cheese to melt and the bread to get crispy. **Do not use foods that can cause illness if undercooked, such as eggs and meats.**

» Note the air temperature at the time you started the project and at 10-minute intervals as the oven heats up. Create a line graph that compares the increase and decrease of the oven and air temperatures over the course of the project.

Project extras

» Include photos of the solar oven in your report.

» Create a chart that compares the pros and cons of cooking with a solar oven.

» Include photos of the sandwich before and after it cooked in your solar oven.

» Research and describe why solar ovens may be of particular use in developing countries.

Writing your report

In many ways, writing the report of your investigation is the hardest part. You've researched the science involved, and you've had fun gathering all your evidence together. Now you have to explain what it's all about.

You are the expert

Very few other people, if any, will have done your investigation. So you are the expert here. You need to explain your ideas clearly. Scientists get their most important investigations published in a scientific magazine or journal. They may also stand up at meetings and tell other scientists what they have found. Or they may display a large poster to explain their investigation. You might consider giving a talk or making a poster about your investigation, too. But however scientists present their investigations, they always write it down first – and you must too. Here are some tips about what you should include in your report.

Some hints for collecting your results

» **Making a table:** Tables are great for recording lots of results. Use a pencil and ruler to draw your table lines, or make a table using a word processing program. Put the units (m, s, kg, N and so on) in the headings only. Don't write them into the main body of your table. Try to make your table fit one side of paper. If you need two sheets of paper, make sure you write the column headings on the second sheet as well.

» **Recording your results:** It is often easy to forget to write down your results as they come in. Or you might just scribble them onto the back of your hand, and then wash your hands! A wise scientist will always make a neat, blank table in their lab book before starting. They will write down their results as they go along and not later on.

» **Odd stuff:** If something goes wrong, make a note of it. This will remind you which results might not be reliable.

» **Precision:** Always record your readings to the precision of your measuring equipment. For example, if you have scales that show 24.6 g, don't write 24 or 25 in your table. Instead, write 24.6 because that's the precise measurement.

Laying out your report

You could use the following headings to organise your report in a clear manner:

» **A title**
This gives an idea of what your investigation is about.

» **Aims**
Write a brief outline of what you were trying to do. It should include the question you were trying to answer.

» **Hypothesis**
This is your scientific prediction of what will happen in your investigation. Include notes from your research to explain why you think your prediction will work out. It might help to write it out as: "I think … will happen because …"

» **Materials**
List the equipment you used to carry out your experiments. Also say what any measuring equipment was for. For example, "scales (to weigh the objects)".

» **Methods**
Explain what you actually did in your investigation.

» **Results**
Record your results, readings, and observations clearly.

» **Conclusions**
Explain how closely your results fitted your hypothesis. You can find out more about this on the next page.

» **Bibliography**
List the books, articles, websites, or other resources you used in your research.

And finally ... the conclusions

There are two main bits to your conclusions. These are the "Analysis" and the "Evaluation". In the analysis you explain what your evidence shows, and how it supports or disproves your hypothesis. In the evaluation, you discuss the quality of your results and their reliability, and how successful your methods were.

Your analysis

You need to study your evidence to see if there is a relationship between the variables in your investigation. This can be difficult to spot in a table, so it is a good idea to draw a graph. You should always put the dependent variable on the vertical axis, and the independent variable on the horizontal axis. The type of graph you need to draw depends on the type of variables involved:

» A bar chart if the results are **categoric**, such as hot/cold, male/female.

» A line graph or a scattergram if both variables are **continuous**, such as time, length, or mass.

Remember to label the axes to say what each one shows, and the unit used. For example, "time in s" or "height in cm". Draw a line or curve of best fit if you can.

Explain what your graph shows. Remember that the reader needs help from you to understand your investigation. Even if you have spotted a pattern, don't assume that your reader has. Tell them. For example, "My graph shows that the soil absorbs heat faster than water". Circle any points on your graph that seem anomalous (too high or too low).

Your evaluation

Did your investigation go well, or did it go badly? Was your evidence good enough for you to support or disprove your hypothesis? Sometimes it can be difficult for you to answer these questions. But it is really important that you try. Scientists always look back at their investigations. They want to know if they could improve their methods next time. They also want to know if their evidence is reliable and valid. Reliable evidence can be repeated with pretty much the same results. Valid evidence is reliable, and it should answer the question you asked in the first place. As before, remember that you are the person who knows your investigation the best. Don't be afraid to show off valid evidence. And be honest if it's not!

Glossary

accurate close to the true value

air pressure force caused by the weight of air pressing down on a given point on Earth; also called atmospheric pressure or barometric pressure

atmosphere layer of gases that surrounds Earth

barometer instrument that measures air pressure

categoric variable that can be given labels, such as male/female

cloud cover amount of the sky that is covered by clouds

collection stage of the water cycle in which precipitation builds up in oceans, lakes, streams, and other bodies of water

condensation process in which water vapour changes to a liquid

continuous variable that can have any value, such as weight or length

control something that is left unchanged in order to compare results against it

convection transfer of heat caused by circular movement of air or water

data factual information

electrophorus device that collects and discharges static electricity

evaporation process in which water changes from a liquid to a vapour or gas

evidence data that has been checked to see if it is valid

heat capacity amount of heat needed to increase the temperature of a substance by one degree Celsius

hypothesis scientific idea about how something works, before the idea has been tested

meteorologist scientist who studies and predicts weather

precipitation process in which water (in the form of rain, hail, sleet, or snow) falls from clouds to Earth

prediction say in advance what you think will happen, based on scientific study

variable something that can change; is not set or fixed

water cycle continuous cycle in which water moves from Earth to the atmosphere and back again

Index